To Your Dog's Health!

To Your Dog's Health!

Canine Nutrition and Recent Trends Within the Pet Food Industry

Mark Poveromo

Poor
Man's
Press

636.7085
P869t

Published by Poor Man's Press
109 Flanders Road, Woodbury, CT 06798

Distributed by Emerald Book Company

For ordering information or special discounts for bulk purchases, please contact Emerald Book Company at PO Box 91869, Austin, TX 78709, 512.891.6100.

Design and composition by Heide Balaban
Cover design by Heide Balaban
Cover photograph Bleacher + Everard

Publisher's Cataloging-in-Publication Data
(Prepared by The Donohue Group, Inc.)

Poveromo, Mark.
    To your dog's health! : canine nutrition and recent trends within the pet food industry / Mark Poveromo. -- 1st ed.

     p. : ill. ; cm.

    ISBN: 978-0-9843017-0-6

1. Dogs--Nutrition. 2. Raw food diet. 3. Enzymes in animal nutrition.
4. Vitamins in animal nutrition. 5. Pet food industry. I. Title.

SF427.4 .P68 2010
636.7085   2009911361
ISBN 13: 978-0-9843017-0-6

Part of the Tree Neutral™ program, which offsets the number of trees consumed in the production and printing of this book by taking proactive steps, such as planting trees in direct proportion to the number of trees used: www.treeneutral.com

TreeNeutral

Printed in Canada on acid-free paper

09 10 11 12 13 14   10 9 8 7 6 5 4 3 2 1

First Edition

This book is dedicated to Drake, my beloved chocolate Labrador retriever. My dog of a lifetime, Drake died at seventeen years of age in September 2007. Some say it was a fluke that he lived so long. I disagree. Caring for Drake was a pleasure, and that care directed me to have a career in animal nutrition. Today I concentrate on educating others about the new and exciting foods and supplements we can give to our precious dogs and cats. (Although this book is written primarily for dog owners, the general principles found here also apply to cats.)

For their assistance and patience, I also dedicate this book to my sons, Mark and Mike; my mom and dad; and the inspiration of my life, my wife, Roxanne.

Contents

Preface

I t has taken me many years to compile the information found within this book, and I believe it will help you provide your pet with sound nutrition. As a result of my undergraduate and graduate studies, my thirst for information about dog nutrition has only intensified. Over the course of many years, during which I cared for thirteen Labs, I wanted to provide the best food available for all of them so they could live long and healthy lives. I was certain plenty of other people felt the same way about their pets. Based on that certainty, I made my decision to open a feed store that would carry only the best dog and cat foods money can buy, not the popular brand-name foods found in most pet stores.

Never complacent where animal nutrition is concerned, I knew I should write about what I have learned regarding animal nutrition. These feelings and experiences provided the additional catalyst for me to write this book.

As you read this, your understanding of basic dog nutrition will improve and become a paramount objective in your life with your dog. So it's up to you. Good luck in your new approach to a healthy diet for your beloved dog.

Acknowledgments

I would like to express my sincere thanks to the many unbelievably talented associates who helped this book come to fruition. Thank you Dean Everard and Katie Bleacher of Bleacher+Everard Photography; I could not imagine doing this without your assistance and professionalism and recommendations. Thanks to Heide Balaban, my incredible layout designer; without you this project would never have been as successful. Thank you to Candace Clark, my "ace in the hole"; through your foresight and talent you have made this book as pleasing to look at as it has been to write. Finally, thanks to all my customers who had faith enough in me to confer about their pets' health matters. If it were not for you, this book would not have happened. God bless you all.

Introduction

My professional career in animal nutrition, breeding, and training has an interesting genesis. In 1979 I was teaching high school physics and environmental science classes, but as the days passed, I knew I needed to supplement my meager teacher's salary of $12,000 a year to support my family of four. I decided to operate a part-time landscaping and lawn maintenance business. My days were long. Sometimes I worked twelve to fourteen hours a day (depending on the time of year) at my various jobs. Moreover, as my years of teaching in an inner-city school accumulated, I began to desire a career change.

Early in my teaching career, I remember thinking that upon retiring after thirty-five years in education I would—with luck—perhaps open up a small business. I wanted a small town atmosphere and community that would support such a venture. Eventually, I decided on the town of Thomaston, Connecticut.

Then, in April 1988, Lady Luck visited me.

Safari Club International selected me as its Teacher of the Year in Connecticut, and as part of the award I had the opportunity to travel to the Grand Tetons and Yellowstone National Park. So it was that while hiking in the Grand Tetons in Wyoming on that exceptional two-week field course my obsession with animal nutrition began. As one of twenty-eight teachers selected from around the country to study the various habits of bears, coyotes, elk, moose, and mountain lions in Yellowstone, I knew I was having the experience of a lifetime. I decided then and there to leave the teaching profession as soon as it was financially possible to do so, to continue my education in nutrition, and to start a dog and cat food business.

After returning to Connecticut with my new calling, I was fortunate to find an eight-hundred-square-foot store in Thomaston called the Outpost Supply, the same building where the Thomaston Feed & Supply, the local feed store, had been located since the early 1900s. There I opened my business as we entered the '90s. (And the addition of chocolate Lab Drake to our household was all I needed to round out my obsession.)

The early days were very trying times. For example, the business might take in only fifty dollars a day in sales. Then misfortune struck in January 1996, when the store suffered a devastating fire that nearly closed down the business. I endured, though, running the business out of two forty-foot storage trailers. Nighttime business hours at the store were the most trying, however; I had to use flashlights for lighting and a ceramic heater to keep my Labs and me warm through the cold winter nights.

Nevertheless, in 1997, after eighteen years of teaching, I decided to leave that profession and devote my energies full-time to the business, the family, and the five Labs we owned: Drake, Jess, Slate, Cider, and Dash. My wife and young sons helped me rebuild the business, along with my nephew Brian and my sister-in-law, Vicki. In 1998 I changed the business name to Thomaston Feed (I had named it Thomaston Feed and Grain in 1995 out of respect for its heritage in the town). With my family's help and under the influence of six more Labs—eleven in all—we were truly a family-run business!

As the years passed, the business grew and managing it became easier. I lost seven of the original eleven Labradors, most to age, a few to unfortunate accidents. The death of one's dogs is always difficult and poignant, but there's nothing like a new puppy to help one forget the losses. Thus it was that in September 2007 my friend and confidant Peter Rothing of Diamond R Kennels in Belgrade, Montana, sent me my then newest Lab, Ruger.

Thankfully, I was fortunate to have Drake and Ruger at the same—though very short—time. Drake was seventeen years old and suffering from acute heart failure. It was obviously time to let him go. He died on September 18, 2007, just five days after Ruger entered my life. I see many of Drake's traits in Ruger; my wife, Roxanne, and I believe Drake's spirit lives on in him. That renews my strength and interest in breeding and training these wonderful dogs. As further evidence of this, we have recently added a Lab puppy, Gunner, to our family. Western-bred (and yet another gift from Peter Rothing), Gunner is the first yellow male I have ever owned.

These incredible animals have inspired and motivated me to write this book.

I hope that as you read through this book you recognize that outstanding nutrition is the foundation of your dog's health. Granted, it does not negate the importance of vet visits, but it does help limit them. Nutrition, therefore, should be a priority of each and every dog and cat owner. For it is up to us toprovide the very best care we can find and afford for these incredible animals.

As Dr. Albert Schweitzer once said, "A man is ethical only when life, as such, is sacred to him, that of plants and animals as that of his fellow men, and when he devotes himself helpfully to all life that is in need of help."

Is It Time for a Change?

S o, here you are, reading this book because you're considering a change to your dog's or cat's diet. You are probably wondering what is the best way to begin.

To simply recommend the best food for your special pet is counterproductive. No food made today is right for all dogs. I have heard many salespeople for dog foods make ridiculous claims as to how perfectly nutritious their traditional food products are for any dog, regardless of the dog's medical conditions. I remember one incident, for example, where a representative for a well-known dog food recommended a significantly high protein diet for a specific diabetic dog. After I looked at the dog's vet records, it was obvious that this food was not at all good for that dog diagnosed with diabetes. To be clear, anyone who makes such statements stretches truth to its breaking point. So, all pet owners must first realize that foods are not created equal, which will become more evident as you read on.

The discrepancies in the alleged benefits of processed dog foods are significant. In evaluating the most important aspects, remember that digestibility is primary. For example, many brands claim upward of 90 percent digestibility of their products. This is actually asserting that any dog, if properly fed, can process or utilize up to 90 percent of the nutrients in their food. But what animal has this capability of processing food so efficiently? Most canine and feline digestive systems cannot utilize 90 percent of any processed foods. The ability of dogs to digest 70 percent is more realistic. Dogs and cats, moreover, digest food at different levels due to many factors—age, weight, and to some extent, breed.

Likewise, pet food companies use the generic phrase "the normal, average dog," which is a very misleading and ambiguous statement at best.

You should never say one dog has the same digestive capabilities as the next, for you need to consider many points to determine what dog food is best suited for your pet—as well as your wallet!

Dog food is customarily prepared in four different ways: fried, baked, pressure-cooked, or dehydrated. Dogs can also eat raw ingredients. The first three methods of preparation use basically the same process, called extrusion. The ingredients are placed in a large vat, mixed together, and pushed out in the shape of the kibble designated by the manufacturer before the food is cooked.

Frying is the most common way pet foods are cooked. Unfortunately, it is not always the best process. You can easily identify whether the dog food you've purchased has been fried by adding water to it and watching to see if the food expands. Know that the fried kibble you see expanding before your eyes will react precisely the same way once it reaches your pet's stomach. This expansion will stretch and, in turn, increase the volume of the stomach, resulting in your pet's increased appetite.

Hint: Choose a baked or pressure-cooked food over fried food. And watch where you shop! Many of the foods found in grocery, department, and convenience stores are fried. It's simple to tell whether the food falls in the baked category: it crumbles easily when squeezed between your fingers. Remember how much easier it is for your dog's digestive system to break down baked food.

However, adding water to the fried food does assist the digestive enzymes (although insignificantly) in the food, making them more viable. So it's a good idea to add water to help the enzymes still present in the food break down that food more efficiently so your dog can digest it.

Today, most pet foods are normally fried at approximately 180 degrees or baked at 220 degrees. Such high temperatures frequently destroy most of the vitamins, minerals, and beneficial bacteria in prebiotics and probiotics. (Prebiotics are nondigestible food ingredients that stimulate the growth of bacteria in the digestive system, which are beneficial to the overall health of the body. Probiotics are live microorganisms [bacteria] that are beneficial to the natural microbial balance found within the small intestine.) I recommend pressure-cooked and baked pet foods (despite the high baking temperatures) over fried food because foods prepared using those two methods do not expand anywhere near the proportions that fried foods do, and they are more easily broken down than their fried counterparts. This is the same, of course, in human nutrition.

Unfortunately, all cooking processes used in producing pet food have a detrimental effect on the beneficial bacteria and digestive enzymes commonly found in meat and vegetables. Therefore, you might consider adding a digestive enzyme mix such as Totalzyme or Nzymes to your pet's food. Among the many enzyme mixes available to the conscientious consumer, choose one that contains the following:

- Protease (helps your dog digest proteins)

- Lipase (helps your dog digest fats)

- Amylase (helps your dog digest carbohydrates)

Additionally, papain, bromelain, cellulose, pectinase, and phytase are excellent enzymes to have in the mix. These enzymes assist your pets in absorbing nutrients and should be staples in their diets no matter what dry food you give them.

Moreover, adding beneficial bacteria, such as varieties of *Lactobacillus* (*L-acidophilus*, *L-bulgaricus*, *L-thermophilus*), *Bifidobacterium*, or *Enterococcus*, will help in nutrient assimilation. These bacteria will also save you money. How, you ask? When you add beneficial bacteria and/or digestive enzymes to your pet's food, your pet's digestive system will absorb and use more of the nutrients in the food. The result is that you will feed your pet less food. This means the pet owner winds up spending less money for far more nutritive food. Isn't that a win-win situation for the pet owner as well as the pet?

What's Out There?

Recently, holistic pet foods have appeared at the forefront of the pet food industry. (The term *holistic* is intended to mean that there is nothing harmful in the food for your pet.) But what appears to be a health food craze has actually been around for about thirty-five years. It all started back in 1974 with a truly revolutionary pet food company called Solid Gold (www.solidgoldhealth.com). Now, we see the "big guns" of the pet food industry (Purina, Science Diet, Nutro, and Iams, to mention just a few) adding holistic pet foods made from all natural ingredients to their inventories as if they had just invented the concept! However, their idea of health food for dogs and cats leaves a lot to be desired.

Here is an abbreviated list of the many "true" holistic dog foods you can choose from. (I provide a brief description of each of these in chapter 12, "What Processed Dog Food Should You Use?" as well as the "points to ponder" [that is, pros and cons] of each.)

- Go! Natural and Now! Grain Free (manufactured by Petcurean)

- Horizon Legacy

- ZiwiPeak

- Taste of the Wild

- Innova and California Natural (manufactured by Natura)

- Weruva

- Pinnacle (manufactured by Breeder's Choice)

- Premium Edge

- Natural Balance

- Fromm

- Orijen

- Mulligan Stew

- Solid Gold

- Merrick

If you decide to give any one of these products or companies a try, remember this important point: switch gradually from one dog food to another. Wean your pet from the old food to the new, which can usually be completed in approximately three to five days.

Initially, always feed your pet less of the holistic pet food than the premium brand-name food you are transitioning away from. You should also rotate protein sources. This means that if you are feeding your pet a chicken-based diet one month, you should try lamb the next month, beef the next month, and so forth. Remember: rotating your dog's food for variety and, more important, its health is vital.

Try to find holistic foods that offer more protein, preferably from meat (percentage wise), than what is generally found in the so-called superpremium pet foods. This percentage, found in the information on the back of the food bag under "Guaranteed Analysis," tends to be around 30 percent protein for holistic foods. Remember, dogs are carnivores and desire meat, not carbohydrates. Examine the food listing for as many meat proteins in the top four ingredients as possible. Always make sure these proteins are specifically spelled out: chicken, lamb, beef, venison, and so on. Then look for nonfragmented grains (preferably no grains at all) and/or fruits and veggies.

The remaining 70 percent is divided among carbohydrates, fat, fiber, and moisture levels. The percentage of carbohydrates varies greatly. Likewise, fat levels can range from as little as 5 percent to 20 percent or higher. Therefore, read the nutrition information and choose your new holistic food wisely. Fiber levels are usually around 4 percent in the better dry foods. Fiber is a transport, which means it quickly pushes the ingested food through the digestive tract. The higher the fiber, the fewer nutrients are absorbed. That's why most vets and nutritionists recommend foods with higher fiber levels for overweight dogs. In simple terms, fiber fools the brain, telling it that adequate amounts of food are present and to continue with normal metabolic rates. Then, as the fiber does its job, the brain senses the loss of food and tells the body to burn fat for the energy it needs. (Isn't science fascinating!) Moisture is simply the amount of liquid still found within the kibble despite the cooking process. Moisture levels in dry foods usually fall around 10 percent.

> **Hint:** Always transition to a new food slowly. It might take as few as three days or as long as a week for your dog to accept its new food. Remember, a dog is a creature of habit, and habits are hard to break.

Today's pet foods tend to be classified according to these four categories:

- Economical—foods that possess nonspecific proteins, fragmented grains, fillers, and by-products; most contain many, if not all, of the commonly identified allergens in dog foods

- Premium—foods that possess more recognizable proteins and grains (albeit fragmented), and a reduction of fillers, by-products, and allergens

- Superpremium—foods that contain specific meats and grains or carbohydrates, with few by-products (some allergens may be present)

- Holistic—foods of human grade, that is, exemplary proteins, whole grains, complex carbohydrates (fruits and vegetables), and none of the commonly recognized allergens; holistic can also refer to raw diets that contain specific meats (including offal and bone), fruits, and vegetables, but no grains

These classifications can often be a bit confusing, however.

As of December 2008, sales of holistic pet foods reached $15 billion. So now the superstores are jumping on the proverbial bandwagon. Thus, consumers are well advised to seek out retailers who will inform them as to the benefits of the fine pet foods to be had, not present them with a sales pitch about what's on sale or what's popular among other customers who buy pet food.

The national pet store chains tend to sell only the big four manufacturers: Eukanuba, Nutro, Purina (Pro Plan, Purina One), and Science Diet. The multitude of pet food manufacturers makes it unfeasible for any store to carry all of the products that are obtainable. Suffice it to say, however, that the best foods are found on the shelves of your independent dog- and cat- food retailer. Thankfully, at these independents you can become educated as to the foods and supplements that will give your much-loved pets the best nutrition.

The best pet foods should display on their bags or cans a list of ingredients that specifies the sources of protein (chicken, duck, beef, trout, etc.). These protein sources should ideally be range fed or wild caught, not farm raised. In today's ever-demanding market with exploding populations, most manufacturers use whatever sources of meat and carbohydrates are readily procurable. Most of the time that means farm-raised animals and fish, which are usually fed foods that contain steroids, growth hormones, and antibiotics. Wild caught is not a perfect food either due to the pesticides and fertilizers that are being used to excess on farms and on most lawns. The best pet food would contain an organic blend of meats, fruits, and vegetables. These are not easily found but are available in your pet specialty stores, although the cost of such may be prohibitive.

Carbohydrates are classified as either complex (fruits and vegetables) or simple (grains). I highly recommend that you choose a grain-free dog or cat food. Also look for these ingredients as you are deciding which product to purchase:

> Chelated minerals—these minerals are bonded to proteins to increase their absorption

> Prebiotics—these nondigestible foods stimulate the growth of beneficial bacteria in the digestive system and keep them healthy

> Probiotics—these dietary supplements help the body utilize foods more efficiently by restoring "friendly" bacteria to the digestive system

All these are vital to have in the food, but always remember that any of these digestive aids are better than nothing. Chelated minerals certainly increase digestibility of whatever food you have chosen, resulting in your dog utilizing more of his food and that food being less taxing to his body. Employing this technique means that energies derived from the food would be available to the other eight systems in his body.

And this translates into your dog having a healthy body and being a happy pet.

3

All Foods Are Not Created Equal

I t's not within the scope of this book to present the actual physical process of food digestion. What you will see throughout the chapters, however, is a word often used to explain how a dog metabolizes its food. That word is digestibility, which plays an immense role in your pet's health. According to *Merriam-Webster's Collegiate Dictionary*, *digestibility* refers both to something's "fitness" for digestion and to the percentage of any foodstuff in the digestive track that is actually absorbed into the body. Manufacturers often use the term in the context of the benefits of specific dog foods and their bioavailability (that is, the ability of the animal to utilize the nutrients found within the food). In a nutshell, *digestibility* is the term that refers to any given dog food's specific

- Ingredients

- Kcals (synonymous with calories)

- ME (metabolic energy) levels

Always keep in mind that "All foods are not created equal," nor are they digested equally.

Consider a bag of generic dog food. If you examine the list of ingredients on the bag, you may be overwhelmed with fat, protein, fiber, and moisture levels, etc. Further examination would indicate kcals and/or ME levels. Most pet owners overlook or even possibly ignore these values. Although these values do not predict the availability of nutrients for your dog, they do provide you with an understanding of the calorie count (for those dogs that need them counted) and the palatability of the food.

Most well-known food manufacturers claim digestibility levels ranging from 70 percent to 80 percent and higher! What the pet food companies mean by these ranges is very confusing. If a food claims to be, let's say, 90 percent digestible, the output of stool should be proportional to intake, which in this case would be approximately 10 percent of the dog's food intake for the day. To simplify this, consider that if your pet is fed two cups of such highly digestible food, the stool should be insignificant. However, that isn't the result for many pets.

Hint:
The time it takes for your dog to digest its food depends on the type of food you feed your dog. Processed (dry) food can take up to four hours or more to be broken down. Canned food can take as much as two hours or more. Raw food can take approximately one hour. Keep these facts in mind, especially if you have a young dog or a puppy.

Consequently, that inflated digestibility pitch from most pet food companies is meaningless. Realistically, dietary intake and output of stool varies significantly depending on each specific dog. Consequently, any product's digestibility number is at most a best-case guesstimate, not anywhere near an accurate prescription. Puppies, for example, are notorious for high stool production based upon dietary intake because their digestive systems are not fully developed or matured. On the other hand, senior dogs' digestive capabilities have diminished with age. The pet food company claims refer to the average adult dog, yet it can be said with confidence that the average adult dog doesn't really exist when such characteristics as age, breed, health, appetite, activity, and so on, are factored in.

It is very important that you, the consumer, make a wise choice based upon your dog's age, breed, and weight—as well as the ingredients mentioned on the bag or can. And when you choose a food for your pet, be forewarned that influences such as the marketing of the product, brand-name recognition, and word-of-mouth endorsements may affect your decision. Consider that most of the brand-name foods (Iams, Nutro, Science Diet, and Purina Pro Plan, among others) spend a lot of their profits on advertising—not the product itself. Some relatively unknown holistic foods (Go or Now, Taste of the Wild, Mulligan Stew, Orijen, and Evo, to name a few) invest a significant amount of their profits in research and development.

Does that mean these generally unknown foods should be at the top of your list? Yes! These less well-known foods elect to put their money into creating a superior product with superior ingredients: fresh meat (not from a rendering plant), organic veggies and fruits, and little to no grains. These vital ingredients provide exemplary digestibility and palatability for your darling pet.

Your choice of food, therefore, should be based upon what's best for your best friend—not necessarily just what's best for your wallet. Take your time selecting your pet's food and you will be rewarded with a healthier, longer-living dog or cat. Although they may not know it, your pets are counting on you.

I'll Have Mine Raw

Despite the multitude of quality dry and canned holistic dog and cat foods now available to consumers, many pet owners have decided to dramatically change what they have long fed their beloved pets. Raw diets have now become firmly entrenched in many canine and feline nutrition circles. Many dog owners around the country understand the benefits of feeding a raw diet to their best friends. However, these pet owners should further educate themselves on the pros and cons of the raw diet.

PROS

Over the past eight years or so, the raw diet has become the topic of heated discussion for vets, breeders, and owners alike. Those who fervently believe in the raw diet remain adamant about its benefits. After all, the digestive similarities between wild coyotes and wolves and our domesticated best friends are well documented. Moreover, the high digestibility of raw food cannot be ignored. Comparatively speaking, the raw diet is about 40 percent more readily assimilated by your dog. By contrast, processed dry foods, depending on their ingredients, are difficult for your pet to process and digest. And we can't forget that raw food is made in predominantly human-grade facilities that have a higher standard of quality control and overall processing and handling than facilities where dry foods are manufactured.

In the past, finding a complete and balanced raw diet has been difficult. Thankfully, since nutrition has become a hot topic in the pet industry, raw food manufacturers are now making complete diets for your dog and cat. Many independent pet feed and supply stores offer complete and balanced raw diets in accordance with the Association of American Feed Control Officials (AAFCO) recommendations. One of the goals of the nonprofit AAFCO is to "provide a mechanism for developing and implementing uniform and equitable laws, regulations, standards, and enforcement policies for regulating the manufacture, distribution, and sale of animal feeds, resulting in safe, effective, and useful feeds." The AAFCO sets the minimum vitamin and mineral standards that all dog and cat foods must have and similarly clarifies standards for other ingredients (such as by-products, fats, and so on) found within commercial products.

The AAFCO considers a dog/cat diet complete if it provides twenty to twenty-six vitamins and minerals, and states that all processed dry and canned foods found in pet stores should contain at least twenty of those twenty-six substances. Remember, therefore, that if you have chosen a raw diet for your pet, you do not necessarily have a complete and balanced feed. Make sure the food container or packaging states that the food meets or surpasses the standards set by the AAFCO for a complete and balanced diet. If the raw food doesn't meet the AAFCO standards, you may need to tweak the formulation based upon the ingredients found within the particular food you purchase. Contact your vet or, better yet, a nutritionist for assistance and clarifications.

Hint:
Always choose a raw food based on its ability to provide a complete and balanced diet. (If you decide to use a raw diet alone you often must augment it in order to provide your pet with the proper vitamin and mineral mix.) Two of the best complete and balanced raw foods out there for you to consider are Vital Essentials (formerly AFS) and Stella & Chewy's brand raw diets.

Among the other substantial benefits that come from feeding raw food to your pets are these:

- Reduction of veterinary visits

- Reduction of stool

- Improved skin and coat

- Reduction, if not total elimination, of eye and ear discharge

CONS

Some traditional veterinarians claim to have seen an increase in a variety of illnesses among dogs that are fed a raw diet as compared to dogs fed processed kibble or cooked diets. These illnesses include, but are not restricted to, pancreatitis, toxoplasmosis, and ulcers. Vets also mention their concerns about the bacteria salmonella and listeria that may be found in raw foods. To date, however, no documented studies have shown an increase in these illnesses or any reported case of infection from those bacteria in dogs or cats. Yes, these illnesses can and do affect humans, but the chances of their being communicated from pet owner to pet are easily eliminated by washing your hands and the food bowl after the feeding.

Is raw for you and your pet? Because such a decision is not easy to make, it should be based all the more so upon nutritive fact and not conjecture. You will be happy to know, in any case, that there are many excellent raw food manufacturers from which to choose. Some of my favorites are

- Northwest Naturals

- Vital Essentials (formerly Animal Food Services)

- Stella & Chewy's

- Nature's Variety

- Primal

For the record, I have been feeding my pets a raw diet for about seven years now and have had tremendous success. Just look at Drake and his seventeen quality years of life.

The Great Maize Debate

A t the very least, I recommend that you consider a dietary change for your pet to eliminate the commonly found allergens in many dog and cat foods. The main culprits are corn, wheat, soy, and brewer's dried yeast, although these are not the only ones! Let's look at the worst offender—corn—in greater detail.

The history of maize—or as we commonly call it, corn—is long and prestigious. The ancient Mayans called corn the giver of life and the food of the gods, and they also believed they were created from it. Among many peoples, corn is one of the most sacred and revered plants. It continues to be the most common ingredient found in premium pet foods today, yet it is widely viewed as the number one ingredient to delete from your dog's or cat's diet.

Here it is necessary to clear up the many misconceptions about corn and provide you with some facts from the most recent scientific studies.

- Corn provides the highest energy content of all grains. When ground, it is also highly digestible (up to 90 percent), whereas ground wheat is 85 percent digestible. However, corn falls behind ground brown rice, which is 99 percent digestible.

- Corn is packed with unsaturated fats and linoleic acid that are good for your pet's skin and coat.

- Corn, in germ form, is an excellent source of fiber and is also the most inexpensive of the generally preferred proteins: fish, chicken, pork, beef, and lamb.

After reading that list of advantages, you might be wondering why, if your pet's food has corn in it, you should be concerned. Here's why I think you should be.

- Corn is one of the four primary allergens in all dog and cat foods and treats. These allergens can result in symptoms ranging from hot spots, ear/eye irritations, and anal gland problems to poor skin and coat condition. (Note that several reactions may occur at once.)

- Corn, as well as other grains, may carry toxins such as aflatoxin, vomitoxin, or mycotoxin. Aflatoxins are naturally occuring products of the fungus *Aspergillus flavus* and *Aspergillus parasiticus*. These toxins, once ingested, attack the liver. Corn treated for aflatoxin is usually sprayed with a liquid ammonia herbicide—something neither you nor your pet should consume.

- Corn also tends to produce a larger volume of stool, and to be less palatable or attractive to a dog's or a cat's taste buds.

Remember that if corn is listed as the first ingredient in a pet food, this indicates it is the most prevalent ingredient, by weight, in that food or treat. Know, too, that corn processed for dog and cat foods is usually of an inferior grade and has, most likely, been treated with pesticides. (This is true for foods ranging in quality from Alpo to Eukanuba.)

Many pet owners ask, "Why do pet food companies use corn instead of or mixed in with meat?" Several reasons underlie this practice, the most obvious one being cost. Corn is a relatively inexpensive food. Since dog and cat food profits are relatively low to begin with, the manufacturers want to increase their profit margins any way they can. Palatability is another reason for its use, for of the numerous grains used in pet foods, corn is more tasty and appealing than wheat and rice are.

If it does not negatively affect your dog or cat, corn is a fine alternative source of protein (albeit vegetable), fiber, and carbohydrate—all in one! Most of you know the benefits of a high-quality protein food source, but few of you realize the vital importance of carbohydrates in your pet's diet. In short, without minimal carbohydrates and fats, proteins cannot be effectively utilized, that is, converted into glucose, by your pet.

Experts agree that the necessary amount of carbohydrate assimilation is usually 5 to 10 percent of the animal's total diet. However, this minimal amount has stirred up many a debate as it applies to dogs. Most people believe dogs are carnivores (meat eaters), but others say dogs are omnivores (meat, vegetable, and fruit eaters). I think of dogs as carnivorous omnivores! Cats, on the other hand, are true carnivores. They metabolize 0 percent of carbohydrates.

In any case, glucose is the fuel for any pet's furnace, and without it our pets will otherwise exhibit lassitude in their daily lives.

Although recent scientific studies show corn to be an inferior protein source better suited for our plant-eating four-legged friends than our carnivore companions, many pets do very well on a high-corn diet.

Hint:
Corn is used as a protein, a fat, and/or a fiber source in all pet foods. In the past you could easily identify those brands that primarily contained corn by their lower price. Today, with ethanol extracted from corn being used as an energy alternative, this is no longer necessarily the case.

But the fact remains that most dogs and cats require animal protein (chicken, beef, lamb, turkey, etc.) more than vegetable protein. Therefore, corn used in a recipe comprised of primarily meat proteins is sufficient for your dog and should be used without any worry, unless an allergic reaction is confirmed. These may include itchiness, hot spots, or flatulence.

Increased stool volume is generally a telltale sign of the appearance of corn in your dog's diet. As a rule of thumb, a dog defecates the same number of times it eats. This may vary somewhat but should not excessively deviate from the rule. You should consider, then, the amount you feed and periodically check the volume of your dog's stool. Doing so may give new meaning to the adage "You get out what you put in."

Although there is no precise formula of food-to-stool ratio, you should be able to recognize excessive stool amounts. If it is excessive, check to see whether your dog's food contains corn and where it is listed within the ingredients. Then decide if it's time to eliminate corn from your dog's diet.

The best pet foods today tend to distance themselves from corn or, at the very least, they use either certified, pesticide-free, organically grown corn or only the gluten of the kernel (the actual protein source in the corn).

If you have a dog with excessive amounts of energy, you would be wise to avoid any foods or treats containing corn or its derivatives. As an important carbohydrate source, corn adds to a dog's potential energy reserves . . . and you don't want that, do you?

A few alternatives to corn for you to consider are quinoa, tapioca, oats, amaranth, and sweet potatoes. Each in its whole form offers a nutritionally superior alternative and is more hypoallergenic. At best, these grains should be pesticide free, organically grown, and of course, free of disease. Remember that as a result of most mass-marketed dog and cat foods using corn and other simple carbs in their ingredients, our dear pets are becoming more susceptible to various inflictions such as ear/eye irritations, anal gland infections, and loss of fur. Always try to choose those foods without the common allergens (corn, wheat, soy, and brewer's dried yeast), or ideally, that are grain free.

Corn will continue to be a widely discussed and debated ingredient in pet diets. If you believe that anything in moderation cannot be that bad for your pet, consider the repercussions of feeding your dog corn-based products the next time you visit your vet because of your pet's food allergy or you need to clean up after your pup!

A significant increase in dog and cat intolerances directly related to high grain (carbohydrate) consumption is now occurring due directly to the inability of pets to digest the high-carbohydrate-driven foods. I have always said, "An educated consumer is one of my very best customers." Educate yourself and choose your dog's food carefully. Remember, a direct correlation exists between proper nutrition and the health of your dog.

Kidney Disease:
An Alternative Approach

A significant variety of foods for dogs—more than two hundred different ones, to date—can be purchased today, and an extraordinary number of them contain these inferior ingredients:

- Animal by-products

- Sugars

- Salt

These ingredients, to name only a few, can and do wreak havoc on our pets' digestive, excretory, and immune systems. Is it any wonder, therefore, that when these foods are consumed, our dogs and cats fall prey to an increase in kidney, liver, and heart ailments?

As I discussed in chapter 5, feeding your dog and cat mass-marketed, carbohydrate-driven foods can cause many adverse reactions—especially to the kidneys. These can and may include excessive weight gain and digestive difficulties (flatulence, diarrhea). Remember, specific diseases need to be attacked in different ways, and diet should be one of your primary tools to prevent illness and to strengthen your pet's immune system. This is particularly true in the case of kidney disease.

Today there is much interest in homeopathic or holistic alternatives to the traditional allopathic (veterinarian-based) treatments, yet once kidney disease is diagnosed many pet owners remain in the dark about homeopathic regimens. Through my many years of studying kidney disease, however, I have found several very promising holistic alternatives for the pet owner's consideration.

I won't elaborate here on the causes of kidney disease or diabetes; rather, I will discuss the alternatives on hand to battle them. (Kidney disease is obviously not the same as diabetes, but the diets to help treat both conditions can be similar.) Remember, diabetic animals have a decreased resistance to bacterial and fungal infections, and as a result can exhibit dermatitis conditions (bad skin and coat). Therefore, you should consider providing your dog with a better diet and supplementing that with vitamins: B_6, B_{12}, C, and the enzyme CoQ_{10}.

Liquid fish oils (omega-3s) and leucine are also excellent supplements to consider. Liquid fish oils are an incredible immune system builder and antioxidant. Leucine is an exceptional amino acid that helps regulate blood sugar levels by stimulating the release of insulin from the pancreas. Leucine's properties also help protect the liver.

In conjunction with a dietary change, always keep your dog's veterinarian and/or nutritionist informed of your dog's dietary intake of food and supplements. These supplements may continually provide alleviation of certain symptoms and may prevent worsening of a condition(s) that results from kidney disease or diabetes.

Always consult with your veterinarian and/or canine nutritionist for professional recommendations. You may also want to search the Internet for additional information about any of the following supplements:

- Ren Suis and Solidago—these supplements are used to detoxify the kidneys

- Renatrophin—a glandular nutritional supplement used to repair the kidneys and make them more efficient

- Bioprin—a Chinese herbal supplement that fights infection and pain in the kidneys caused by the Lyme spirochete

- Lyme Colostrum—a supplement that enhances the immune system of your pet

Take heart: if your pet is diagnosed with kidney disease it is not necessarily a death sentence. The starting point for overcoming a disease such as this continues to be your pet's diet. In other words, what your dog eats is the most significant matter for you to consider.

To choose the right food for your dog, you must accurately determine the actual amount of protein in your dog's diet. If you are concerned about this for weight management or kidney-related issues, examine the back of the bag where the protein, fat, fiber, and moisture levels are stated. Bear in mind that the protein level is usually given as a minimum amount. Because dogs with kidney disease have difficulty breaking down substantially high protein levels, you need to exercise caution in making your selection.

So, just how do you determine what the correct protein level for your dog is?

Look on the back of your dog's food bag or can and note the protein level. Then look at the moisture content (usually around 4 percent). Subtract the stated moisture level in the kibble from 100 percent, and then divide the stated protein level in the food by that result.

To illustrate, let's use a dog food with a protein level of 26 percent and a moisture level of 4 percent as an example. After we subtract the moisture level from 100 percent (which results in the number 96), we divide the stated protein level of 26 percent by 96 to get the actual level of protein in your dog's food. Twenty-six divided by 96 equals 27 percent, the maximum recommended protein level for most pets.

This example reveals that a food may be too high in protein for your dog if it needs a special kidney diet. Moreover, many veterinarians and nutritionists still recommend a maximum protein level of 18 percent to 20 percent in the commercial food that is fed to a diabetic dog or one inflicted with kidney disease. Therefore, you should always confer with your vet or pet nutritionist for their recommended maximum protein intake for your dog.

These commonly recommended lower protein levels, however, create a problem: the ability of your dog (or any dog) to adequately break down inherently poor protein sources (corn, animal by-products, etc.). When you choose a commercially prepared dog food for treatment of kidney disease, always give first consideration to those foods that avoid meat and plant by-products (animal digest, rice, bran, etc.) and choose a low to zero simple-carbohydrate-driven food (corn, rice, wheat, etc).

Also you may consider a highly digestible protein source as well as a diet driven by complex carbohydrates (vegetables and some fruits). Remember, many fruits and vegetables—for example, apples, peaches, watermelon, carrots—are naturally high in the natural sugar fructose for most dogs. Although these are quality foods, they are too high in fructose for most dogs. Limit their place in your dog's kidney diet.

Hint: Always consider a holistic supplement if your pet suffers from kidney disease. Quantum Herbal Products offers an excellent product called "Kidney-Bladder," a low-alcohol tincture to be used in conjunction with your dog's dietary change.

Finally, with the many diseases threatening our dogs, you may want to consider some of the many home-cooked diets designed for your dog's nutrition and health. They may well prove to lengthen your dog's life and well-being. (In the next chapter, "Be a Top Chef for Your Dog," I provide several recipes for conscientious pet owners to make for their dogs that are suffering from kidney ailments.)

Kidney diets, however, tend to result in a higher digestible protein (around 27 percent or lower) and a higher digestible complex carbohydrate formulation. Grains, therefore, should be eliminated from your pet's diet.

Lyme disease, rampant where I live in Connecticut, can also stress your pet's kidneys. The reduction of deer habitat has resulted in an increase in urban deer populations. As a result, Lyme disease—one of the leading causes of kidney disease or kidney failure in our pets—is spreading at an astronomical rate through deer ticks! Many dog owners think Lyme disease is not a problem because they believe that the Lyme disease vaccine provided by their veterinarian protects their pet. However, the vaccine itself is not as effective as the medical community suggests. Consider the fact that the Lyme bacteria spirochete is the same spirochete as in the human disease syphilis, and no cure for the latter yet exists.

Nevertheless, most veterinarians strongly recommend the Lyme vaccine. Whenever vets have questioned me about this inoculation, my response has been a question of my own: If there is such an epidemic of Lyme disease (as well as ehrlichiosis, anoplasmosis, and heartworm disease), why are the populations of coyotes, foxes, and wolves continuing to thrive? Boy, that really ticks them off! I wonder what your vet's response to this would be.

It's a simple answer, really. The diets of feral (wild) canines are unprocessed and balanced. Raw, hunted food is, by far, what keeps these animals healthy and thriving. The diet of a dog's distant and not-so-distant relatives is what is best for a dog. So, before you buy a commercially sold, processed dry dog food consisting of approximately 40 percent meat and 55 percent carbohydrate, consider a change to something more nutritious. Or better yet, cook for your pet—for your own peace of mind as well as for your pet's health. If you don't prize your dog's health, who will?

Be a Top Chef for Your Dog

Quite a number of holistic vets and practitioners—myself included—believe that home-cooked meals for your dog are an excellent alternative to most store-bought foods. The renowned veterinarian Martin Goldstein wrote what I consider to be an essential read for all caring pet owners, *The Nature of Animal Healing*. Dr. Goldstein is one of the most sought-after speakers with respect to animal health.

In his book, Dr. Goldstein introduces pet owners to alternative ways to supplement their pet's diet to treat specific disease(s). He is a staunch proponent of raw food for dogs and cats. If you can't feed your pet the best food (that is, raw), he would recommend home cooking, followed by canned, and finally dry kibble(s). However, the preponderance of foods available to the pet owner are precisely those inferior food types. Why? Because they are convenient. We have become a society fixated on keeping it simple. After all, there's nothing easier than opening a bag and pouring its content into your pet's bowl. But thankfully, not all pet owners do this. Are you one of those who is treating your pet to a better, healthier diet?

Many pet owners have opted to cook for their pets, which is excellent for pets as long as the diet is complete and balanced. What follows are several easy-to-make recipes that I have experimented with over the years, some of which your dog with kidney-related problems or diabetes should absolutely love and benefit from!

Cooked Diet Recipe #1

A kidney-friendly diet for an 80-pound adult dog's daily feeding.

1 cup of meat or fish (turkey or pollock)

1½ cups of low-fat cottage cheese

2 hard-boiled eggs

1 cup of brown rice or 2 boiled sweet potatoes w/skin

1–1½ cups of vegetables: broccoli or zucchini, squash or asparagus (use carrots sparingly)

4 Tbsp of sardine oil (to be added after steaming)

1–2 Tbsp granulated garlic

1 tsp sea salt

1.5 oz of liquid Fido nutrients (vitamin/minerals, digestive enzymes, and much more) from the makers of K-9 (www. LiquidHealthinc.com) to meet vitamin/mineral standards as set forth by the AAFCO

Chop all ingredients into small pieces to create a casserole and steam for approximately 5 minutes. Remember: Don't overcook!

This will make enough for one feeding.

Vary the proteins every other week or so, and change your vegetables weekly, using a combination of any two. Intermittently, change over from the brown rice to sweet potatoes.

Remember, variety is the spice of life for dogs as well as for you. After all, you wouldn't want to eat the same thing day after day, week after week, would you? Your dog will love this diet and all its variations!

The cost of this food for a week (that is, seven feedings) should be around $29.00 (2009 pricing), which is not inexpensive but is less than a raw diet—which can cost upward of $4.50 a day—or some dry diets.

Cooked Diet Recipe #2

A low-protein diet for dogs that weigh up to 30 pounds and have kidney problems or diabetes.

2–3 hard-boiled eggs

2 cups of brown rice (barley, millet, or sweet potato)

1½ cups of green beans or yellow squash

2 Tbsp canola oil

½ tsp sea salt

1 tablet of calcium carbonate (Tums unflavored)

A multivitamin and mineral supplement, preferably liquid

Steam all of the components for about 3 minutes; don't overcook. This recipe will take about half an hour to prepare.

Divide the mixture by two for twice-a-day feeding.

The cost of this diet should be approximately $20.00 a week (2009 pricing).

Cooked Diet Recipe #3

**A low-protein diet for dogs that weigh around
50 pounds and have kidney problems or diabetes.**

3 hard-boiled eggs

3 cups of whole oats (not microwavable)

3 cups of kidney beans

3 cups of steamed vegetables (broccoli, zucchini,
or yellow squash)

2–3 Tbsp liquid fish oil (hoki, sardine, or salmon),
after steaming

1 tablet of calcium carbonate (Tums unflavored)

Steam all of the components for about 3 minutes; don't overcook. This diet will take approximately half an hour to prepare.

The cost of this food per week should be approximately $22 to $25 (2009 pricing).

Cooked Diet Recipe #4

For a 70-pound dog's daily feeding
(not recommended for dogs on protein-restricted
diets because of their kidney problems or diabetes)

1¼ cups of meat (beef, pork, chicken, duck, or fish)

1 hard-boiled egg

¼ cup of brown rice or 1 boiled sweet potato

1 cup of vegetables, preferably green and fresh
(use carrots sparingly)

1 Tbsp sardine oil (to be added after steaming)

1 tsp garlic

⅓ tsp sea salt

liquid multivitamin and mineral supplement

Chop then mix all ingredients and steam for approximately 3 minutes.
Remember to add the liquid multivitamin/mineral mix after cooking.

This will make enough for one feeding and takes about half an hour
to prepare.

The cost of this food per week should be about $25 to $30 (2009 pricing)
depending on the protein used.

Please remember that acclimating your dog to a home-cooked diet is the same as changing from any one type of food to another. Make the transition slowly. On Day 1, the mix in the food dish should be about 75 percent of your pet's old food and 25 percent of the new (home-cooked) recipe. On Day 2, try a 50-50 mix. Watch for digestive upsets (such as diarrhea); if there are no signs of an inability to digest the new recipe, the mix on Day 3 should be about 25 percent old food and 75 percent home cooked. The meal on Day 4 should be 100 percent home cooked.

If at any point in the transition your dog suffers from diarrhea, return to Day 1 ratios and repeat the process, slowly reaching the complete acclimation to the new diet.

Hint:
Did you know that a home-cooked diet is the second easiest diet for your dog to digest? Only raw food is easier. A cooked diet can take as little as two hours for your pup to digest. This user-friendly fact is invaluable, especially when you start to house-train your best friend!

I know many of you have very busy schedules, so you'll love this great time-saving idea: cook a week's worth of meals at one time. Devote four to five hours one day a week to cook and divide portions that you store in the refrigerator. This will allow you simply to feed and go!

Before converting to home cooking or making any dietary change, always have your veterinarian run blood tests on your dog. The table that follows provides acceptable blood levels of various substances for the dog that has been diagnosed with kidney disease. Knowing these ranges will help you understand the urgency for treatment, diet, and/or supplementations for your dog.

Blood Count Reference

(Ranges are given in milligrams per deciliter [mg/dl])

Glucose....................................70–138

Urea nitrogen.........................6–25

Total protein...........................5–7.4

Alkaline phosphate.................5–131

Calcium..................................8.9–11.4

Phosphorous...........................2.5–6

Bun (creatine).........................4–27

Potassium...............................3.6–5.5

Magnesium.............................1.5–2.5

Creatine..................................0.5–1.6

Use this as a reference against which to compare your dog's results provided by its vet.

If and when you decide to create a diet for your dog with kidney failure or disease, always remember to concentrate on foods that are moderate to high in fat, for it is important that your dog maintain a healthy weight to battle this disease. Also keep in mind that foods high in fat normally provide calories low in phosphorous. This is very important to know, for phosphorous can become another enemy in dogs with kidney disease.

When you cook for your dog, remember that raw lamb and pork are high in fat. Beef is also another good choice if your dog is not allergic to it. You may also use turkey or chicken, but try to use the dark meat, which is higher in fat than the white meat. Dairy products are known to be high in fat, but they are also high in phosphorous, so use them sparingly.

It is very important to understand the dangers of phosphorous. If your dog's phosphorous levels are high (above 5 mg/dl), add calcium to its diet. This will help bind the phosphorous and flush it out of the dog's system. You can also decrease phosphorous levels in your dog's diet by using the required dosage of potassium citrate. These levels are based upon the dog's weight.

Other examples for adding calcium to your dog's diet include, but are not restricted to, ground egg shells, Tums antacid tablets (with calcium carbonate), or the prescription medication Calcitriol (a form of vitamin D). As always, seek assistance from your veterinarian or nutritionist when making this decision.

Reduce, if not totally eliminate, sodium from your dog's diet by using sea salt instead. You also should increase potassium levels in your dog as it fights kidney disease with a potassium chloride supplement.

Finally, stay away from high-protein treats and snacks. Consider sweet potato fries (homemade, of course) or, when available, fresh raw vegetables (green beans, zucchini, etc.), instead. (Note that dogs with kidney-related problems have trouble keeping weight on. Enough calories and carbs each day are obviously crucial and beneficial for these dogs.)

As I mentioned in previous chapters, I'm a strong believer in supplementing any and all diets. Here are some well-researched and accepted choices for supplements for animals that have kidney problems. Consider introducing at least one, but preferably more, to your dog's diet. (The normal recommendation for a dog that weights more than forty pounds is to use the same dosage, as stated on the back of the bottle, as that for an adult human. For dogs that weigh less than forty pounds, use one-half the stated dosage for an adult human.)

- Garlic

- Hawthorn

- Ginkgo biloba

- B vitamins

- Burdock

Note: Check with your veterinarian or nutritionist if you have questions about supplementation dosages.

The Ugly *C* Word

For humans and their pets alike, no other disease foretells an early death as cancer does. Cancer is also so diverse that it is difficult to list its many variations. As an owner of a pet that had this dreadful disease, I know that cancer is extremely adept at using carbohydrates to promote its growth and acceleration. And despite the advent of better foods and supplements, cancer's ugly presence is still bedeviling our pets.

One of the many possible reasons why cancer still threatens people and their pets is the presence of environmental toxins that we are exposed to daily. Synthetic fertilizers in our yards, cleaning liquids in our homes, and air pollution, among others, continually threaten our well-being. Genetics also play a role: is your dog possibly prone to cancer? Statistically, the following breeds of dogs have been genetically predisposed to this horrible disease:

- Airedale terrier

- Beagle

- Bouvier des Flandres

- Boxer

- Bulldog

- Bull terrier

- Doberman pinscher

- German shepherd

- Golden retriever

- Great Dane

- Great Pyrenees

- Labrador retriever

- Rottweiler

- Saint Bernard

To read a more comprehensive list of dogs prone to cancer, go to www.canismajor.com/dog/cancer1.html.

Given the poor-quality plant ingredients—pesticide-treated grains, fruits, and vegetables—contained in so many commercial dog foods, and the even more disgusting quality of the animal protein sources many manufacturers use, is it any wonder our pets are susceptible to cancer and other diseases?

Here's a fact that should sicken the animal lover in all of us: The protein sources found in most mass-marketed pet foods are purchased from rendering plants. There are 250 or so such plants in the United States, and they are commonly referred to as the "silent industry." (I can't help but think that companies who buy the by-products of these rendering plants are thankful so many people are oblivious to their existence.) In large vats, sometimes referred to as "huggers," these plants grind and filter animal tissues prior to deep-frying them. Each year these salvage centers for dead, dying, diseased, and drugged animals process more than 12.5 million tons of fat and meat wastes!

A U.S. Department of Agriculture report stated that approximately 10 billion pounds of meat, bone, blood, and feather meal were produced in the year ending 1996. Approximately 50 percent of these by-products ended up in brand-name pet food! Hard to swallow, isn't it? But the bad joke is really on your pet.

This is further proof of why it is so important to feed your pet a quality food. Remembering these nightmarish statistics will help you resist the convenience of shopping in a grocery store for your pet food. You will be happier because your pet will be healthier and also happier.

Most if not all homeopathic vets and nutritionists now recommend home-cooked diets and a strict regimen of supplements for dogs that have cancer. If you are concerned about a lump or a change of character in your dog or cat, seek immediate medical attention for your pet. It is always best to assume the worse about your pet's health and therefore to address problems and treatments early.

At the very least, to help prevent cancer in your dog you should evaluate what you are feeding it. Consider changing to a holistic diet of grain-free food or one with as few carbohydrates as possible. Why? Because many of the pet foods available—even super-premium, and holistic—are carbohydrate driven. I tell customers who come into my store saying they have found a bag of dog food that looks good and contains specific proteins (chicken, beef, lamb, turkey, etc.) and carbohydrates (rice, potato, barley, etc.), in that order, they should look at the price. If they believe that they are buying, say, chicken and rice, yet they see a price tag of $34.99 or so, they need to beware! Never have I seen, anywhere, a bag of dog food consisting primarily of chicken with vegetables/grains for so little money. Most likely, this food is a multi-vegetable/carbohydrate with only a little chicken.

Hint: Always consider adding a holistic supplement if your pet suffers from cancer. One excellent product I recommend is called "Immuno Stim'R," a low-alcohol tincture from Azmira to be used in conjunction with your dog's dietary change.

Economically speaking, there is no way pet food manufacturers can afford to put the protein source stated on the bag as the primary ingredient after cooking. The obvious reason is that the primary source(s) of protein, whether that is chicken, lamb, beef, fish, etc., is composed of upward of 70 percent moisture (water). Cooking removes a large percentage of that, which dramatically changes the volume of meat actually found within the bag of food. If manufacturers listed "after cooking" volumes, that bag of food would be priced closer to $75.00 or so!

The dog owner must also consider as clean a food as possible. By that I mean pet food that is as free of allergens (corn, wheat, soy, brewer's yeast) as possible, and with as few (or no) grains whatsoever. A food with multiple proteins listed at the beginning of the ingredient list is great. All of the ingredients listed on the bag should be as low in the percentage of carbohydrates as possible. Many grain-free dry diets boast a breakdown of 70 percent meat and 30 percent carbohydrates. This formulation is, obviously, more highly digestible than the grain-driven varieties.

Still need help deciding? Ask your pet nutritionist or your veterinarian.

Be a Top Chef
for Your Dog with Cancer

When they are suffering from cancer, dogs require specific dietary supplements and/or changes to their usual diets. Thus, with that in mind, many conscientious pet owners today are deciding to cook for their ailing dogs and cats.

Here are two recipes (followed by a list of holistic supplementations I recommend and have used with my dogs) to help you begin that shift to preparing meals for your pet.

Homemade Cancer Diet Recipe #1

For a 30-pound dog's daily consumption

4 oz ground beef/turkey/chicken (steamed), whatever you wish to use on any given day. Or you can use 4 to 6 oz of fish. (Be mindful that cold-water fish, such as salmon, trout, or sardines, are better than fish that live in warm water, such as tuna.)

2 whole carrots (either boiled and then chopped or raw grated pieces) or look into the supplement Olewo (dehydrated carrot pellets), a fantastic dehydrated carrot product from Germany. Use as directed in substitution for fresh or frozen.

1 cup of spinach (fresh cooked or frozen)

4 Tbsp green bell pepper (chopped and steamed, but optional because some dogs don't like peppers)

4 broccoli flowerets (boiled and then chopped)

2 tsp flax oil or sardine oil, add after steaming

1 clove raw garlic (crushed and added before serving)

1 tsp dry, ground ginger (added before serving, but optional because some dogs won't eat ginger)

You may want to consider adding some apple cider vinegar instead of the ginger. I always prefer it in liquid form. Also consider adding a liquid vitamin/mineral supplement to your dog's diet. Liquid Health's Fidonutrients is a great product to consider.

You can steam all the vegetables together and then add them to the protein source afterward. This will take you approximately 40 minutes and will cost approximately $30.00 a week depending on your choice of meat (2009 pricing).

Homemade Cancer Diet Recipe #2

For a 70-pound dog's daily consumption

1 cup of tofu or Quorn (soy substitute made of mushrooms) or 8 egg whites

2 cups of lentils or kidney beans

3 cups of boiled (with skin on) sweet potatoes

2 Tbsp hoki, sardine, or salmon oil, add after steaming

$1/3$ tsp sea salt

1 Tbsp liquid multivitamin, add after steaming

Combine all ingredients and steam for approximately 3–5 minutes. This diet should take approximately 30 minutes to prepare and cost about $35.00 a week (at 2009 pricing).

Remember, both of these recipes can be easily adjusted to feed any size dog. If, for any reason at all, you are unsure as to your dog's dietary needs, contact your veterinarian or pet nutritionist.

In conjunction with these cancer diet recipes, I strongly recommend the following supplements to your dog's daily diet. (Note: Adjust the supplements appropriately for your dog's ideal weight, not its actual weight. The supplements listed here are for a 70-pound dog.)

- Vitamin E (1000 IU per day)

- Selenium (300 mcg per day)

- Beta-carotene (Vitamin A)
  up to 2,500 IU per day per pound of food, or 2 raw carrots, grated, if the dog likes them

- Quercetin (500 mg per day)

- Omega-3 fatty acids

- Gamma-linoleic acid

- Coenzyme Q_{10}

Antioxidants are also good for preventing and treating canine cancer and should be, at the very least, included with some kind of multivitamin (liquid preferably). Antioxidants prevent free radicals from damaging healthy tissues. Free radicals are widely accepted as being a major cause of aging and the development of symptoms leading to cancer, strokes, and heart disease. Arguably the best antioxidant for your dog (or cat) is omega-3 (found in fish oils).

If you have a hard time finding the aforementioned supplements you can also use these other supplements (more readily obtainable) for your dog with cancer:

- Echinacea. This plant is an immune-system booster. You can find echinacea in health food stores in several forms: tablets, tinctures, capsules, and extracts of dried or fresh roots. Although most American doctors aren't familiar with echinacea, researchers in many other countries have studied its beneficial effects. Follow adult dosing directions.

- Cat's claw. The herb *Uncaria tomentosa* comes from Peru and is used to treat arthritis and cancer. Studies have confirmed that it has antioxidants and immune-enhancing properties. For small dogs, use one-quarter the adult dosage, and for medium dogs use half.

- Pau d'arco. An extract from the inner bark of Tabebuia (also known as Taheebo) trees in South America, Pau d'arco contains lapacho and other phytochemicals that produce anti-cancer and anti-inflammatory results. For small dogs, use one-quarter the adult dosage, and for medium dogs use half.

Hint:
I usually set aside half a day (four hours or less) to prepare a week's worth of meals for my dogs. I freeze the individual portions in Ziploc storage bags and warm them before serving so each dog's olfactory sense is stimulated.

- Shark cartilage. This product possesses angiogenic properties that reduce blood vessels in tumors. You can use from 1,000 to 2,000 mg of shark cartilage per day, depending on your dog's weight. Check for recommended dosages with your veterinarian, nutritionist, or oncologist.

- Beta-glucan. This complex sugar is found in the cell walls of many medicinal mushrooms, such as maitake, as well as in oats, barley, and baker's yeast. It has been used to treat cancer in humans and pets alike.

Today, many Eastern alternative medicines are being used separately as well as in conjunction with traditional treatments. Acupuncture may relieve pain and provide an analgesic effect without the side effects of such drugs as steroids. It may likewise stabilize the function of the adrenal gland and increase the secretion of endogenous corticosteroid. Electrical acupuncture may also improve muscle strength and reflex activity and help relieve muscle spasms after operations. A course of acupuncture usually involves several treatments. If the process doesn't show results in three to five treatments, then it probably won't work for your pet. Your veterinarian may be able to refer you to a veterinary acupuncturist, or try www.aava.org.

Remember, despite its horrifying reputation, cancer has been treated and beaten by veterinarians using conventional and holistic treatments. Don't give up.

Alternative Foods for Your Dog

A s the search for better nutrition for dogs continues to grow, more and more people are deciding to cook for their pets because the benefits of the home-cooked diet are so numerous. Don't be worried that you don't have the time to be your dog's top chef. I have recommended and developed many cooked diet recipes for my customers that would yield enough food to feed a dog for a week and take less than two hours to prepare. When you decide to cook for your dog, however, remember to make sure the diet you prepare is as complete and balanced as you can possibly make it.

As you begin to perceive the long-term benefits of the recipes provided in this chapter, always remember to rotate them, for the sake of both variety and health. The belief in the past has always been to provide a structured diet for a dog every day, sometimes twice a day. Wild (feral) dogs and cats, however, are opportunistic hunters. They never, or at least very rarely, eat the same thing every day. Vary your dog's diet and you will see it become more interested in the food and, just as important, less likely to develop intolerance toward what it eats.

I have heard time and time again: "My dogs never had problems before with their food. What's happened?" The simple answer is that as dogs (and humans too) age, their once strong digestive, immune, respiratory, and other systems become less effective. Normal age-related attrition—together with the effects of environmental toxins, poor diet, and overvaccinating—has taken its toll. One of the nicest things you can do for your pet is to give it home-cooked meals packed with love.

Below are a few more recipes for home-cooked foods you can alternate preparing to provide a healthy alternative to a store-bought, processed diet.

Home-cooked Diet Recipe #1

For a 35-pound dog's daily consumption

1¼ cups of meat (beef, pork, chicken, duck, or fish)

1 hard-boiled egg

¼ cup of brown rice or 1 boiled sweet potato

1 cup of vegetables, preferably fresh greens, but frozen is okay (use carrots sparingly)

1 Tbsp sardine oil (to be added after steaming)

1 tsp garlic

⅓ tsp sea salt

liquid multivitamin and mineral supplement, as directed

Steam all of these ingredients after chopping them into small pieces, and serve as a casserole. This will take approximately 40 minutes to prepare.

Cost of this food per week should be about $25 to $30 (2009 pricing).

Vary the protein from week to week and frequently change the vegetable source. Use a combination of any two proteins and alternate between brown rice and sweet potato each week. Again, variety is the spice of life!

Home-cooked Diet Recipe #2

For a 65- or 70-pound dog's daily consumption

3 cups chicken, turkey, or beef (as lean as possible), or pollock, cod, or any other low-fat white fish fillet

2½ cups of zucchini and/or sweet potato

1¾ cups of celery or summer squash

2 Tbsp sardine oil (to be added after steaming)

1 tsp garlic

¼ tsp sea salt

liquid multivitamin and mineral supplement, as directed

Wash the potatoes well and cut them into two-inch-thick round slices. Simmer for 45 minutes to 1 hour. Wash and similarly slice the zucchini. Wash and cut up the celery or squash. Steam or cook these vegetables until very tender. Note: You may substitute other vegetables (broccoli, for example) periodically, but avoid high-sugar varieties such as carrots and peppers. Stick with leafy green veggies (but not green beans) as much as possible.

If using pollock, cod, or any other low-fat white fish fillet, cover it with water in a frying pan and poach it until the fish is white and flaky.

Mix all ingredients together until well blended. (You can use a blender or stir by hand with a spoon.) This will give you approximately 8 cups of food. Depending on the size of your dog, this can give you upward of three days' worth of feeding. This recipe remains fresh for three days in the fridge. Freeze the remaining portions in individual storage bags.

The cost of this food should be around $35–37 a week (2009 pricing).

If you have been feeding kibble, please remember that kibble has many more calories than does home-cooked food. You will need to prepare at least 25 to 50 percent more home-cooked food than kibble until you are sure your dog's weight is holding where you want it. Remember to feed your dog based on its ideal weight, not what it weighs when you first change over to the new diet.

Hint:
Remember, variety is indeed the spice of life. I constantly change my dogs' diets. I even use a dry kibble sporadically. My dogs never know what they will be getting, and they never walk away from their feed. Allowing your dog a varied diet will certainly all but eliminate its fussy tendencies.

Choose your protein carefully. Make sure your dogs are not allergic to the specific protein you have selected. Some signs of an allergic reaction can be hot spots, itchiness, ear/eye irritations, or anal gland problems. If you see any of these symptoms consult with your vet or nutritionist.

NOTE: Home cooking is very rich. Because you have been feeding your pet commercial dog food, you will need to switch to the new diet very slowly so the Duke or Duchess in your house won't have an attack of diarrhea. Start with three-quarters of your commercial dog food and one-quarter of the home-cooked diet for a few days. Then 50 percent commercial food and 50 percent home cooked for a few days. Then one-quarter of your dog's original food and three-quarters home cooked for a few days, and then after a few more days switch over completely to the home-cooked diet. Make certain the stools are somewhat firm before you move to the next level.

Enzymes: Nature's Catalysts

Enzymes, commonly called the body's workers, are one of the newest attributes to join the pet food industry's list of must-have ingredients. As a way of understanding the multitude of enzymes that can or should be used in your dog's or cat's diet, I will classify enzymes into two types:

- Digestive Enzymes

- Food Enzymes

DIGESTIVE ENZYMES

Digestive enzymes, manufactured in your dog's or cat's organs, are secreted by the stomach, the pancreas, and the small intestine. Technically, digestive enzymes are considered to be metabolic because their primary purpose is to help your dog digest food.

Digestive enzymes produced by the stomach and the pancreas include:

- Protease (breaks down proteins)

- Amylase (breaks down carbohydrates)

- Lipase (breaks down fats)

- Pectinase (breaks down pectins/sugars commonly found in the cell walls of plants)

Because these enzymes deal with digestion, they can be supplemented from an outside source. Adding these can increase your dog's ability to utilize more of its food.

FOOD ENZYMES

Food enzymes exist naturally in raw food, but processing (cooking) methods tend to destroy some, if not all, the enzymes normally found in a food.

Even though digestive and food enzymes tend to serve the same process, that is to digest foods, they differ in that food enzymes exist in pet foods as opposed to being manufactured in the animal's body.

The four digestive enzymes listed earlier can also be found in good bacteria, which process proteins, carbohydrates, fats, sugars, and fibers, and thus help your pet maintain a good digestive tract. When you examine the contents of your next bag or can of dog or cat food, keep in mind that it should contain these four genera of bacteria:

- *Lactobacillus acidophilus*—commonly found in the small intestine; inhibits bad bacteria from multiplying

- *Streptococcus thermophilus*—commonly found in the small intestine; aids in the relief of lactose intolerance because it produces lactase, the enzyme needed to break down dairy products

- *Enterococcus faecium*—commonly found in the small intestine; has proved to be effective in the treatment of diarrhea

- *Bifidobacterium*—commonly found in the large intestine; produces lactic and acetic acid, which effectively lower the pH of the intestinal tract; as an immune system stimulus, is an excellent warrior in destroying cancer cells

Referred to as "probiotics," these powerhouses need carbs if they are to function efficiently. Make sure your dog's food sources contain adequate amounts of carbohydrates.

Some other examples of good bacteria to look for are

- *Aspergillus oryzae*

- *Bacillus subtilis*

- *Aspergillus niger*

- *Lactobacillus casei*

If you are uncertain whether your dog food possesses enzymes and/or beneficial bacteria, look for any or all of the following in the list of ingredients: lipase, protease, amylase, trypsin, and catalase. These enzymes are commonly found in such protein sources as beef, chicken, lamb, and pork. Though your dog's food may contain one or more of these proteins, this does not guarantee that your pet will be getting these catalysts in sufficient quantity to increase the digestibility of its food.

Why? Because the high temperatures at which the food is processed basically destroy most of the benefits of the vitamins and minerals, as well as these enzymes. Therefore, if these enzymes are listed individually on a bag or can of dog food, you are most likely looking at a fine food for your pet.

You may also see one of many plant enzymes listed on a quality bag or can of dog food. Examples of these plant enzymes include—but are not restricted to—papain, bromelain, actinidin, and ficin. Such enzymes help to break down proteins, carbohydrates, and fats, and they can be found in fruits and vegetables. If these are found in your pet's food, you can rest assured you are looking at a quality food.

Hint: Several fine products are available for supplying the enzymes your pet needs. Green Dog Naturals' "Whole Dog Daily" is arguably my favorite. Digestix from Kala Health Products is another fine choice. Adding a digestive enzyme mix to your dog's diet can help in so many ways, especially if your dog exhibits a loose stool.

It is believed that up to 70 percent of your pet's internal energy is used to digest foods that do not contain enzymes or that contain them in insufficient amounts. (The worst culprits are dry or canned pet foods.) Not supplementing your dog's diet with enzymes can strain its immune system and make it more susceptible to disease. If the pet's body has to work harder to provide digestive enzymes, then it has far less time to replenish those enzymes organically.

65

What Processed
Dog Food Should You Use?

The question this chapter asks you to consider is highly subjective. As I mentioned earlier, the best foods available tend to be in small, independent local pet supply or feed stores. Yes, your veterinarian does carry pet foods, but those are often foods with limited quality ingredients. Grocery, department, and convenience stores are definitely places where you should *not* look for your beloved pet's food.

Thus, I recommend that you think about the following options as you strive to improve your dog's diet. Although these brands of dog food are available in only select locations, you will likely find a store carrying many of them near you.

1. Breeder's Choice, based in California, has a fantastic line of holistic and superpremium dog and cat foods and treats of varied protein and carbohydrate sources. They offer some of the best baked and pressure-cooked lines available today. The quality of this food, as well as their manufacturing facility, is top-shelf. Their AvoDerm and Active Care lines of products contain approximately 40 percent meat and 55 percent carbohydrate. The Active Care line is a fine alternative for dogs in any stage of life, especially those with arthritis. Some of their other lines are

   - AvoDerm Natural and AvoDerm Baked (chicken, lamb, or trout), available in puppy, senior, and "lite" varieties

   - Active Care (chicken or lamb)

- Pinnacle (trout, duck)
- Pinnacle Peak (holistic grain-free diet), an all-life-stages diet that boasts an approximate 65 percent meat and 35 percent carbohydrate formulation; a great food at a very reasonable price

2. Canidae has been one of the industry leaders over the past years. This American company's lines are all approximately 45 percent meat and 50 percent carbohydrate. Canidae offers, among others,

- All Life Stages (chicken, turkey, duck, or salmon), available in a grain-free version
- Chicken and Rice
- Lamb and Rice
- Beef and Fish

3. Diamond brand dog and cat foods, based in Missouri, is another excellent source of holistic and superpremium pet foods. The company offers four different product lines, the first three of which are 45 percent meat—always fresh, never frozen—and 50 percent carbohydrate.

- Diamond Naturals (chicken, lamb, or beef), available in puppy, senior, and large-breed varieties); boasts more than 150 quality-control checks for this line of food as well as their others.
- Premium Edge (chicken or lamb), available in puppy, senior, and large-breed varieties; Healthy Weight 1 (a weight-reduction food line) and Healthy Weight 2 (a weight-management food line) are both superlative and economical.
- Chicken Soup for the Dog Lover's Soul (chicken, turkey, duck, or salmon), available in puppy and large-breed puppy, adult and large-breed adult, senior, and "lite" varieties. They also have a nice line of holistic treats!

- Taste of the Wild (bison, venison, wild fowl [quail, turkey, duck, and chicken], or salmon) provides a grain-free diet of exceptional protein sources. (The guaranteed analysis boasts a 70 percent meat and 30 percent carbohydrate formulation.) Undoubtedly Taste of the Wild is Diamond's best line of dog food and is formulated for all life stages. Its high-quality ingredients and high digestibility all but eliminate the need for age-specific diets.

4. Weruva brand is another excellent line of holistic dog and cat foods. The company boasts a diet that is 70 percent meat and/or fish and 30 percent carbohydrate. At present, Weruva products are available in canned versions only. These pet foods are proposed human grade, a great point to consider. At the time of this writing, Weruva had just introduced a new line of products called Best Friends Food. Their spectacular BFF cat food line is available in 3 oz. and 5.5 oz. sizes; Weruva's dog food varieties are available in a 13 oz. size. Weruva foods are a must for pet owners to consider.

5. Fromm, based in Wisconsin, offers two main lines of healthy pet foods from which to choose:

   - Fromm Gold (chicken, salmon, duck, or pork), available in puppy, adult, and senior varieties. This line is about 45 percent meat and 50 percent carbohydrate.

   - Holistic Surf and Turf (fish or chicken), formulated for all stages of life. This grain-free food is made according to a recipe that calls for 70 percent meat and 30 percent fruits and vegetables.

6. Nature's Variety, a corporately owned American company, makes exceptional pet foods and treats. Both of Nature's Variety's lines— Prairie and Instinct—are formulated for all stages in a dog's life, which means you can feed your puppy, adult, and senior dog any of their versions. This is possible because the high-quality ingredients promote high digestibility, which all but eliminates the need for age-specific dog foods.

- Prairie (beef, chicken, lamb, venison, or salmon). Each mix is approximately 45 percent meat and 50 percent carbohydrate.

- Instinct (chicken, duck and turkey, or rabbit). This grain-free line boasts a mix of 70 percent meat and 30 percent fruits and vegetables.

7. Natura, a U.S. company with a great reputation, is best known for its Innova and California Natural lines of dog and cat foods and treats.

Hint:
With so many wonderful pet foods to choose from, make your selection based on these factors. Where is the food made? Are the ingredients from quality sources? Is the food a wise choice for your pet based upon its needs? If the answers don't satisfy you, you need to buy your pet food elsewhere. Remember, opinions are rampant; get the facts.

- Innova (chicken, turkey, duck, or salmon). Each of these varieties is made up of about 50 percent meat and 45 percent carbohydrate.

- California Natural (lamb or chicken). These two varieties consist of 50 percent meat and about 45 percent carbohydrate, including brown rice.

- Evo (red meat or white meat). Formulations are about 70 percent meat and 30 percent fruits and vegetables. This superb grain-free line is also formulated for dogs at all stages of life.

8. Petcurean, a Canadian company of great integrity and reputation, is arguably producing one of the most highly digestible foods you could want for your dog or cat. Their high-quality foods are available in two different blends: Go and Now, which can be found at select stores. In my opinion, they are well worth locating and buying.

- Go! Natural (chicken, turkey, duck, or herring). The combinations of 70 percent meat and 30 percent fruits and vegetables provide some of the highest kcal counts of all holistic dog foods.

- Now! Grain Free (turkey or duck), available in puppy and adult varieties. This grain-free food also boasts 70 percent top-quality meat and 30 percent fresh fruits and vegetables

9. Orijen is another exceptional Canadian company that boasts a formula of 70 percent meat and/or fish and 30 percent fruits and vegetables. Orijen comes in both puppy and adult varieties. Their six-fish (salmon, herring, freshwater cod, lake trout, lake whitefish, and walleye) product is excellent. They have recently introduced a Regional Red version, a red meat formulation boasting wild boar, and free-range lamb and heritage pork. Regional Red is an incredible addition to an already superb line. Orijen's senior line is also a great choice for your older dog. The company's high level of quality control has certainly helped it to earn a high reputation. Orijen also offers a great cat food. I highly recommend this line for your cherished dog or cat.

10. Solid Gold, based in El Cajon, California, boasts that in 1974 it began the holistic dog and cat food craze. Its food averages approximately 45 percent meat and 50 percent carbohydrate in six of their seven different varieties. Solid Gold also has an impressive line of treats and biscuits, as well as a canned-food diet.

Their dry foods are as follows:

- Hund-n-Flocken (lamb "dog flakes" for adult dogs)

- Hundchen Flocken (lamb "dog flakes" for puppies)

- Holistique Blendz (a fish and carbohydrate line)

- MMillenia Beef & Barley

- Wolf King (bison, salmon, and carbohydrates for large-breeds)

- Wolf Cub (bison and salmon [hypoallergenic] for puppies)

- Just a Wee Bit (bison and salmon [hypoallergenic] for toy and miniature breeds)

- Barking at the Moon, Solid Gold's version of a grain-free dog food. This is an exceptional food of approximately 70 percent meat/fish (beef and whitefish) and 30 percent fruits and vegetables. A very palatable alternative to the other grain-free foods, Solid Gold continues to be a great choice for your dog and cat.

11. Mulligan Stew, manufactured in Jackson Hole, Wyoming, offers sublime dry and canned dog and cat foods. Designed and created by a biochemist and naturopathic healer, Mulligan Stew is a relatively new food supplier (at the time of this writing) with five varieties: chicken, beef, salmon, turkey stew, or its fabulous Jackson Hole stew (buffalo, beef, fresh cabbage, horseradish, among other ingredients). Their oven-baked dry food line is also exemplary. With proteins available in fish, chicken, and lamb versions, they're a marvelous choice for your dog. These highly digestible foods that dogs love are a must for your pet's pantry.

12. Natural Balance is produced by an American company whose dog and cat foods (and treats) are a welcome alternative to the grain-free diets often found in your veterinarian's office. They are a one protein (45 percent), one carbohydrate (50 percent) limited-ingredient diet. The three varieties they offer are venison and sweet potato, duck and potato, and fish and sweet potato. The same limited-ingredient diet comes in both a biscuit and a canned-food option. Natural Balance also offers organic as well as vegetarian diets.

13. ZiwiPeak from New Zealand offers an air-dried food and treat line for your dog or cat that boasts a grain-free high-meat (90 percent) and ultra-low-carbohydrate (10 percent) diet that is extremely palatable. The splendid varieties include venison, venison and green lipid

mussel, lamb, or beef, all of which contain perhaps the best poly-unsaturated oil on the market—hoki fish oil. Albeit a little pricey, ZiwiPeak is one of the best foods for your pet. The company motto, "Raw without the thaw," says it all, and the benefits of a raw diet in dehydrated form are vital to your pet's health.

14. Horizon Legacy dog and cat foods, a division of Horizon Pet Foods, is made in Saskatchewan, Canada. This company is another great new food purveyor for the conscientious pet owner to look at. They offer a high-protein, high-fat line of pressure-cooked foods, with multiple protein sources as their primary ingredients and no grains.

These are but a few of the great holistic pet foods available for the health-conscious pet owner to select from. Ask your vet, nutritionist, or independent retailer for other healthy alternatives.

Your Fussy Dog

Don't our pets always challenge us regarding their food? Sometimes, no matter what you offer to your dogs, they put up their noses and walk away. What should you do?

This is an important question because an appetite loss can be a sign of underlying health problems. Therefore, check with your vet if your dog's appetite is suppressed for an extended period of time. Once the vet has examined your dog and given the okay to stimulate its appetite, you can try one or more of these simple tips.

Besides serving a totally home-prepared diet, which most dogs seem to love, you may perk up your dog's appetite simply by warming food up to room temperature or slightly higher—causing the aromas to become more apparent to your older or younger dog's olfactory senses.

You may also try topping commercial fare with one or more of the following:

- Quality cheese (sliced or grated), such as Parmesan, pecorino, etc.

- Granulated garlic (not powder)

- Canned gourmet cat food or dog food (95 to 100 percent meat: for example, Evanger's or Merrick brands)

- Chicken (or beef) broth or gravy (low-salt to no salt)

- Canned tuna with its liquid (preferably water)

Always remember to rotate these ingredients and use sparingly. Do remember, if you are already feeding your dog a dry diet and just want to stimulate its appetite, try changing or making additions to the daily feeding. However, these toppings should not be introduced in the food solely because the food you normally serve is not balanced; rather, you should use a mixer or topper with your dog food choice to create a canine cuisine your fussy pet will eat.

Our pets are, I believe, somewhat psychic. They just seem to know that Mom or Dad will cave in and give them what they want. Well, at least to some degree!

Many times a finicky dog is not born that way; the pet owner creates the finicky eater. I have never had a finicky cat or dog. When all my dogs first became part of my home (perhaps I should say when I first became part of their home!), I immediately began to train them to sit and wait to eat. I'd have them sit and stay in place for a second and gradually increased the sit time. After I released them, they ate with vigor. If they didn't finish their breakfast or dinner in the allotted time (five minutes was the longest time period), I picked up their dishes and they wouldn't eat again until the next meal. Believe me, they learned very quickly: "When Daddy tells me to sit, I'll sit. When Daddy tells me to eat, I am going to eat!"

Hint: Always warm your dog's food prior to serving. Dogs have limited taste buds but an exemplary olfactory sense. In fact, dogs are driven by their sense of smell. By simply warming their diet, you will help them find their food to be more attractive.

(Remember that dogs do not reason as humans do. They will not starve themselves. As always, however, if this training does not have your dog eating in a reasonable period of time, consider seeking medical attention for your dog.)

In my home this practice worked and continues to work. Try it. You will be happy with the results.

Vaccines and Other Treatments

A s with the discussion concerning raw diet feeding, there has never been so heated a topic as alternatives to vaccinations and parasitic treatments for your dog. You most likely know how your vet feels. Nevertheless, there are other considerations.

Today many holistic veterinarians are educating their customers as to the benefits of limiting canine vaccinations. Every month, it seems, you receive postcards and phone calls from the vet reminding you to schedule appointments for proper vaccine treatments. In fact, most vets and breeders recommend the first set of vaccinations be administered to your pet when it is around eight weeks old. I have chosen, however, to limit my dogs' vaccines.

One of the most important nutrients for a puppy is its mother's milk (colostrum), and the puppy's health is undeniably based on the antibodies it absorbs from the colostrum. Therefore, nursing puppies don't need vaccinations at such an early age. I also limit, if not totally disregard, those vaccines for parasitic infestation: Lyme, fleas, ticks, etc. Instead, my regimen includes an all-natural flea and tick repellent called Grr-Lick and a supplement—Immuno DMG from U.S. Animal Nutritionals—that builds the immune system.

I stop all vaccines after the first set of shots for all of my dogs and have had significant success with other means of disease prevention generally handled by vaccination. I do not believe in playing health roulette with my dogs. Therefore, I supplement their food with

- CoQ_{10} (100–300 mg per day)

- Colostrom (follow dosage on bottle)
- Glucosamine, Chondroitin, and MSM (methylsulfonylmethane) (follow dosage on bottle)
- Liquid vitamin and mineral mix (per weight of your dog, follow dosage on bottle)

I always recommend liquid supplements. Whether your pet requires a multivitamin or a thyroid supplement, consider introducing it in liquid form, which is by far more readily absorbed in your dog's system. This regimen, along with a raw diet, has contributed significantly to the longer-than-average lives of some of my Labradors. Remember, there are many supplements available to pet owners, so research the company, the ingredients in the product, and the possible side effects of such a supplement, assuming there are any.

Are these practices of mine right for you and your pet? If in doubt, always research the matter and discuss your findings with the professionals: your veterinarian and/or nutritionist. There are several pet chat rooms on-line that provide a great pro and con for just about every consideration. Checking these out can help you decide what paths you will choose in the quest for Bowser's (or Fluffy's) health.

Instead of an annual inoculation, some veterinarians now offer tittering, a test that checks for residual antibodies in your pet for a specific disease, antibodies that exist because of your puppy's absorption of its mother's milk and/or earlier vaccines.

Throughout my eighteen years in this business, no question has been asked of me more often than that regarding the need of heartworm medications and treatment. Here, too, I have always been a proponent of the holistic approach, and many a veterinarian has raised an eyebrow upon hearing my belief! The particulars of my beliefs, and the success of my approach, however, are easily verifiable and speak for themselves.

Simply speaking, heartworm disease is a geographical and seasonal disease. This means the disease is restricted to those regions where the ambient temperature remains above 60 degrees for thirty consecutive days. If this does not occur, the maturity of the mosquito larvae (heartworm disease carrier) cannot manifest, which all but eliminates the need to treat your dog for heartwormyear-round. Share this with your veterinarian and see if he or she concurs. If not, you have a decision to make.

I have never treated my dogs for heartworm, but I have always supplemented their immune systems with their raw diets. To date, after eighteen years of raising and breeding Labrador retrievers, none of my dogs has had heartworm! These holistic approaches have not resulted haphazardly. Despite my success, however, you need to be fully educated about heartworm disease in order to make a sound decision. When you think you have decided what to do, confirm your decision and concerns with your vet or nutritionist.

Hint:
Thankfully, vets seem to be proposing fewer protocols and vaccines. Remember, your dog's immune system is the key. Prior to choosing a regimen of vaccines, consider giving your dog an immune system booster to help minimize your dog's potential negative reactions to vaccines. Look for products that contain any or all of the following: red clover, blue violet, garlic, echinacea, and vitamins B$_6$ and C (especially for puppies and senior dogs). These are excellent supplements to give to your much-loved pet(s).

You may have noticed that I have not recommended any particular food or supplement. You should refer to chapter 12 for a list of manufacturers of premium pet foods. The following is a list of manufacturers who, in my opinion, produce excellent supplements:

- U.S. Animal Nutritionals

- Nupro

- NaturVet
- Standard Process
- Quantum Herbals
- American BioSciences
- Green Dog Naturals
- Aloha Pharmaceuticals

These are not the only manufacturers of supplements, of course, but I know that each of these companies offers a wide variety of supplements for just about any affliction your cat and dog may have.

Even though I believe that pet owners should supplement the daily food of their dogs (and cats), I refrain from recommending a specific manufacturer's supplement because many may not be readily procurable. Internet searches will help you determine which supplements are available and right for your pet. Your research, in conjunction with proper guidance from your veterinarian and/or nutritionist, should guarantee the proper regimen for your dog's health.

In any case, try to work your way through the massive amount of information concerning vaccination and supplementation without falling into the hands of what I call the dreaded "two Cs": confusion and contradiction.

If you succeed in being decisive and consistent, thus avoiding the two Cs, I know your dog's health will benefit from your discoveries.

Conclusion

Throughout this book I have attempted to present information that is accurate and easy to understand. Moreover, I encourage you to search the Internet and other resources to find answers pertaining to your questions regarding the general well-being of your dog. Then, once you've made your decisions, confirm them with canine professionals and you will be even more confident about your finds.

Many fine books have been published on dog and cat nutrition, and you should read as many as you can to expand your knowledge. If we choose to be pet owners, we owe it to our pets to provide them with the best care available.

As Dr. Albert Schweitzer said, "The purpose of human life is to serve and to show compassion and the will to help others." I believe these "others" are not only humans but also our pets, who are in many ways some of our best companions. I believe, too, that what you have read here is but the beginning of one of life's wonderful experiences, the care of your beloved pet.

About the Author

Mark Poveromo was part of the "system."

He was a physics and environmental science teacher who liked his job and was good at it, so good, in fact, that Safari Club International named him the Connecticut Teacher of the Year in 1988. Yet he knew he wanted more. "When I retire," he kept telling himself.

During a trip to the Grand Tetons, where he observed wild animals in their natural habitat, Mark discovered his calling—two decades ahead of his scheduled retirement. He began to develop a plan for amalgamating his expertise as a nutritionist, his love of animals, and his desire to be his own boss. What followed were a lot of long nights juggling a duel career: teacher by day, retailer of holistic pet foods by night. A lot of family support in minding the store. Too many start-up days at the end of which he confronted a "dysfunctional" cash register. (What else would you call $39 in sales as the day's take?) And a near devastating fire that would have provoked a lesser man to call it quits.

Fortunately for thousands of pets and their masters (a sometimes debatable role reversal), Mark persevered. For while he had seen his dream come true, he had yet to live it, yet to realize its full potential.

Then came the day when Mark had to decide if he was "just" a very good public school teacher or someone whose passion and true calling was in the business he was building from the ground up. He wanted both, but knew he had to make a choice. He ultimately abandoned the security and demands of his day job, "the system," and put all of his time, energy, and whatever resources he had left from the fire into Thomaston Feed.

The fast-growing retail business for holistic pet foods was on its way to becoming the largest of its kind in the Northeast United States.

Then "disaster" struck again when Mark was swindled out of thousands of dollars by a charlatan builder. Weeks of waiting turned into months of waiting. Finally, his pre-fab building arrived; it's just that it was not the building he had ordered and it was lacking the crew required to literally put all of the pieces together.

Once again, Mark persevered. He eventually recouped what was his, and Mark was back on track.

Six months later, near disaster struck—again. This time, it took a crew of firefighters, police, and medics to pry Mark out of the wreckage of a highway automobile accident that a lesser man might not have had the fortitude to survive.

Mark viewed it as yet another wake-up call: Better write "that book." The one that had been rumbling around in his head and heart for years but which he never had gotten around to writing. Too busy teaching and training (except now his "pupils" were four-legged and tended to have their "parents" tag along to "school"). Too busy building Thomaston Feed. Too busy raising his beloved Labs, as many as eleven at one time.

To Your Dog's Health! was Mark's therapy as he recovered from the pain of being a too trusting visionary and the pain of a near fatal car accident.